12/03

Medieval World

Women and Girls
in the Middle Ages

Kay Eastwood

Crabtree Publishing Company

www.crabtreebooks.com

Crabtree Publishing Company

www.crabtreebooks.com

PMB 16A, 350 Fifth Avenue
Suite 3308
New York, NY 10118

612 Welland Avenue
St. Catharines
Ontario, Canada
L2M 5V6

73 Lime Walk
Headington
Oxford 0X3 7AD
United Kingdom

Coordinating editor: Ellen Rodger

Series editor: Carrie Gleason

Designer and production coordinator: Rosie Gowsell

Scanning technician: Arlene Arch-Wilson

Art director: Rob MacGregor

**Project development, editing, photo editing,
and layout:** First Folio Resource Group, Inc.: Erinn Banting,
Tom Dart, Jaimie Nathan, Debbie Smith, Anikó Szocs

Photo research: Maria DeCambra

Prepress: Embassy Graphics

Printing: Worzalla Publishing Company

Consultants: Isabelle Cochelin, Department of History, University
of Toronto; Joseph Goering, Department of History, University of
Toronto

Photographs: Archivo Iconografico, S.A./Corbis/
magmaphoto.com: p. 7 (bottom); Art Archive/Biblioteca d'Ajuda
Lisbon/Dagli Orti: p. 19 (bottom); Art Archive/Bodleian Library
Oxford/Bodley 264 fol 172v: p. 15 (bottom); Art Archive/Bodleian
Library Oxford/Ouseley Add 24 folio 55v: p. 28; Art Archive/
British Library: p. 11 (top), p. 14; Art Archive/Cathedral Treasury
Aachen/Dagli Orti: p. 18; Art Archive/Médiathèque François
Mitterand Poitiers/Dagli Orti: p. 22; Art Archive/Musée Condé
Chantilly/Dagli Orti: p. 23 (left); Art Archive/Musée Thomas
Dobrée Nantes/Dagli Orti: p. 31 (right); Art Archive/Museo de
Arte Antiga Lisbon/Dagli Orti: p. 19 (top); Art Archive/Private
Collection Paris/Dagli Orti: p. 30; Art Archive/University of
Prague/Dagli Orti: p. 9 (bottom); Bettmann/Corbis/
magmaphoto.com: p. 9 (top); Bibliothèque Nationale, Paris,
France/Bridgeman Art Library: p. 4; British Federation of Master
Printers, UK/Bridgeman Art Library: p. 27 (top); British Library/
Add. 24098 f.18v.Min: p. 10 (top); British Library, London, UK/
Bridgeman Art Library: p. 21; British Library/Harley 4431 f.4:
p. 31 (left); British Library/Kings 9 f.64v: p. 20 (top); British
Library/Royal 15 E.I f.170: p. 15 (top); British Library/Royal 16
F.II f.137: p. 23 (right); British Library/Royal 20B XX f.7: title page;
Historical Picture Archive/Corbis/magmaphoto.com: cover; Bob
Krist/Corbis/magmaphoto.com: p. 27 (bottom); Erich Lessing/
Art Resource: p. 6; Musée de l'Assistance Publique, Hôpitaux de
Paris, France/Bridgeman Art Library: p. 20 (bottom); Musée
Condé, Chantilly, France/Bridgeman Art Library: p. 7 (top);
Musée Guimet, Paris, France/Bridgeman Art Library: p. 29
(right); National Gallery, London, UK/Bridgeman Art Library:
p. 26 (right); Newark Museum/Art Resource, NY: p. 29 (left);
Scala/Art Resource, NY: p. 11 (bottom); Snark/Art Resource, NY:
p. 25

Illustrations: Katherine Kantor: flags, title page (border),
copyright page (bottom); Alexei Mezentsev: pp. 12–13; Margaret
Amy Reiach: borders, gold boxes, title page (illuminated letter),
copyright page (top), contents page (all), pp. 4-5 (timeline), p.5
(both), p.8, p.10 (bottom), pp.16-17 (all), p.21 (bottom), p.24 (both),
p.26 (bottom), p.32 (all)

Cover: A lady-in-waiting delivers a book to a group of
noblewomen. Only wealthier women in the Middle Ages
learned how to read and write and could afford expensive
handmade books.

Title page: A queen had several ladies-in-waiting who traveled
with her, helped her dress, and played music to entertain her.

Published by
Crabtree Publishing Company

Copyright © 2004

Cataloging-in-Publication Data
Eastwood, Kay.
 Women and girls in the Middle Ages / Kay Eastwood.
 p. cm. -- (Medieval world series)
Summary: Describes the roles and duties of women and girls of all social classes
during the Middle Ages, looking at such areas as medieval dress and beauty,
women's rights, and women of power in Europe and other lands. Includes
bibliographical references and index.
 ISBN 0-7787-1346-6 (RLB) -- ISBN 0-7787-1378-4 (PB)
 1. Women--History--Middle Ages, 500-1500--Juvenile literature. 2.
Women--Europe--Social conditions--Juvenile literature. 3. Girls--History--Middle
Ages, 500-1500--Juvenile literature. 4. Girls--Europe--Social conditions--Juvenile
literature. [1. Women--History--Middle Ages, 500-1500. 2. Middle Ages. 3.
Civilization, Medieval.] I. Title. II. Series.
 HQ1143.E18 2004
 305.4'09'02--dc22
 2003018228
 LC

Table of Contents

Medieval Society

The period in history called the Middle Ages stretched from 500 A.D. to 1500 A.D. in western Europe. It was a time when people who ruled, called the nobility, fought one another for land and power. The nobility included kings and queens, lords and ladies, and warriors who fought on horseback called knights.

Most people in the Middle Ages were peasants. Peasants farmed nobles' land in return for small plots of land of their own. There were also **merchants**, who made and sold goods in towns and cities, and people who devoted their lives to God. The main religion in Europe during this time was Roman Catholicism, a denomination, or branch, of **Christianity**.

▶ *Some women and girls in the Middle Ages learned trades. This woman was a painter. Her male assistant helped her by mixing paint colors.*

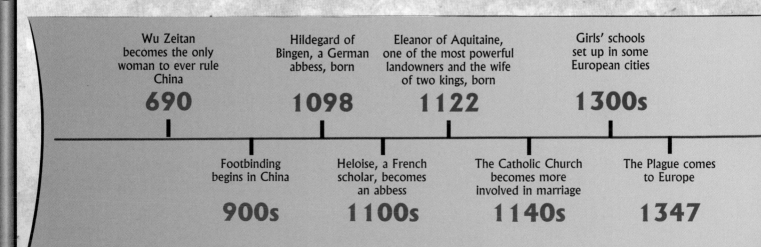

Wu Zeitan becomes the only woman to ever rule China	Hildegard of Bingen, a German abbess, born	Eleanor of Aquitaine, one of the most powerful landowners and the wife of two kings, born	Girls' schools set up in some European cities
690	**1098**	**1122**	**1300s**
Footbinding begins in China	Heloise, a French scholar, becomes an abbess	The Catholic Church becomes more involved in marriage	The Plague comes to Europe
900s	**1100s**	**1140s**	**1347**

▲ *In the Middle Ages, women from places as different as Europe, Asia, Africa, and India made important contributions to their society, both inside and outside the home.*

Women's Roles

The kind of life medieval girls and women led depended on where they lived, how wealthy their families were, and if they were unmarried, married, or if their husbands had died. Many young married women were mothers by the age of fifteen. They also ran the household, helped their husbands with their jobs, and sometimes had businesses of their own.

In the Middle Ages, girls and women had fewer opportunities than men to hold jobs outside the home and become leaders in the community. In spite of this, some women were great achievers, working as writers, artists, doctors, warriors, and even rulers.

▼ *Kings and great lords held the most power in the Middle Ages. Peasants had the least power.*

◀ *King*

◀ *Great lords*

◀ *Lesser nobles*

◀ *Knights*

◀ *Peasants*

Christine de Pizan becomes the first known woman to earn a living writing books
1389

Joan of Arc leads the French to victory over the English in the Hundred Years War
1429

Books written about how women should manage a household
late 1300s

Isabella I, queen of Castile and Aragon, born
1451

Noblewomen

Noblewomen and girls, called ladies, came from families with a great deal of land, wealth, and power. They usually married men from equally powerful families.

Many noblewomen lived in castles, which were large buildings of wood or stone that protected noble families in times of war. People thought that the most important role of a noblewoman was to have children, especially boys, to carry on her husband's family name and to **inherit** his lands.

Girls from noble families usually married when they were around the age of thirteen or fourteen. Many noblewomen had a baby every year from the time they married until they were in their mid-30s.

▲ *Most servants in the castle were men. They looked after the lord, served meals, and entertained guests at feasts. Noblewomen had their own female servants to help them dress and take care of the children.*

Running the Castle ▶

Noblewomen also ran the castle's household. They supervised cooks and other servants, arranged large feasts for guests, ordered supplies from the nearest town or city, and made sure that bills and servants were paid on time. Noblewomen also took care of the **manor** when their husbands were away fighting. They supervised the farming, collected **rents**, and listened to the complaints of people on the noble's lands. If the castle was attacked while her husband was away, the lady defended it.

Queens

When a king died, his eldest son usually inherited his kingdom. In some countries, such as England, if a king did not have a son to take his place, his daughter inherited the kingdom and became queen. Her husband, usually another powerful noble, became king and ruled the country for her. A queen sometimes ruled when her husband was away at war. She also acted as a regent for her son, ruling in his place if he was made king at a very young age. Some queens continued to help rule after their sons took the throne.

▲ *Isabella of Castile inherited the Spanish kingdom of Castile from her father. In 1479, she married Ferdinand, the king of neighboring Aragon, but continued to rule her large kingdom on her own.*

Women in Towns

The main job of townswomen was to look after the family home by cooking, supervising servants, and raising children.

Some townswomen made cloth for wealthier families' clothes. Women called hucksters went from house to house selling items such as chickens, cheese, salt, flour, oats, firewood, and used clothing. Other women had their own businesses, such as preparing dinners for people who did not have kitchens or brewing a weak alcoholic drink called ale and selling it from their homes.

▼ *Most houses in towns were built on top of the family workshop. These houses were very narrow and were built of* plaster *and wood or of stone.*

Learning a Craft

Many townswomen helped run the family business. They learned their husband's or father's craft, such as baking or dyeing cloth, by watching them at work and helping out. Often, the men of the family made the goods and the women sold them at the market or from their homes.

Guilds

In the Middle Ages, merchants and craftspeople who made or sold the same kinds of goods belonged to organizations called guilds. Guilds set the prices of the goods, made sure that all their members produced items of good quality, and cared for guild members who were sick and unable to earn a living. Most guilds had only male members. Sometimes, the widow of a guild member took her husband's place in the guild after he died and continued his trade.

In the larger cities of London in England, Paris and Rouen in France, and Cologne in Germany, women ran silk guilds. Highly skilled women and girls spun silk into thread, then wove it into fabric or made it into ribbons and lace. There were also guilds for women who **embroidered** headdresses, bags, and gloves with silk threads.

▲ *A disease called the Plague killed more than one third of Europe's population between 1347 and 1350. Many workers in cities died. Afterward, women were able to find better jobs and ask for better wages.*

▶ *This woman helps her husband, who is a banker, by counting customers' gold.*

Peasant Women

Peasant women and girls lived in the countryside, in villages surrounded by farmland. Their homes, which usually had only one or two rooms, were either built of stone or from a framework of wood and woven twigs, called wattle. The wattle was filled with daub, a mixture of mud, straw, and animal dung.

In the center of the main room was an open fire over which women cooked. They made simple meals from foods they grew in their gardens, such as onions, leeks, peas, beans, apples, pears, and cherries. They baked bread in the lord's ovens, since most peasants did not have ovens at home. They paid the lord with whatever they had, including freshly baked loaves.

▲ *In the later Middle Ages, peasants had large homes with fireplaces instead of open fires. The men chopped wood for the fireplace, and the women and girls brought the wood inside.*

▶ *Peasant women got together to comb and clean sheep's fleece for wool, weave cloth, sew, and wash clothes in the village stream.*

Farmwork

Women and girls helped out with the farmwork, feeding the chickens and pigs, collecting chickens' eggs, milking cows, sheep, and goats, and shearing sheep. They also weeded the fields where crops grew, picked out stones, and planted seeds. Some peasant girls worked in the lord's manor house, cooking, spinning wool, and washing laundry. Others helped their mothers look after the younger children.

▼ *Peasant women wore simple clothes made from rough linen and wool. They tucked their skirts out of the way when working in the fields.*

Having Fun

Noblewomen and townswomen enjoyed many activities in their free time, while peasant women only took a break from their busy lives on Sundays, religious holidays, and festivals.

May 1 was May Day, a festival that welcomed spring. In some English villages, the prettiest girl was chosen Queen of the May and was decorated with a crown of flowers.

On May Day, peasant women danced around a maypole decorated with ribbons.

Women in towns spun wool to make beautiful dresses and embroidered small tapestries, belts, and other items.

Playing games, such as chess, and musical instruments, such as lutes, were favorite noble pastimes.

Townswomen gathered in taverns to eat, drink, and visit with friends.

Noblewomen hunted on horseback in the forests surrounding the castle.

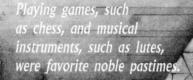

Townswomen went to markets to shop for food, spices, clothing, and other items for their homes.

Getting Married

In the Middle Ages, girls were supposed to marry. Whom they married and how old they were when they married depended on how wealthy their family was.

Choosing a Husband

Girls from noble families and wealthy families in towns usually married men their parents chose for them. Marriages were arranged to bring important families closer together. Love was rarely taken into account.

Less wealthy girls in towns usually chose their own husbands. Towns were full of young men who had moved there from the countryside to work as servants, laborers, and **apprentices**. Peasant girls also chose their husbands, whom they often met while working in the fields.

▲ *Noblemen and ladies often got to know one another by spending time together in the castle's quiet gardens.*

The Dowry

All brides brought a sum of money and possessions, called a dowry, to the marriage. The possessions included items such as cloth, pots, linen, and farm animals. The girl's family usually provided the dowry, which was her share of the family inheritance. If a girl had a large dowry, many men wanted to marry her, and her family usually chose the best match. Noble girls or wealthy girls in towns married around the age of fourteen. Peasant girls often married in their late teens or early 20s because they had to wait until their parents had enough money or land for a dowry. Poor girls who worked in towns also married later, often in their early to mid 20s, because they earned their own dowries, which took many years.

The Wedding Ceremony

In the early Middle Ages, all a couple had to do to become husband and wife was say "I do" to each other. This showed that they both agreed to the marriage. They could say these words in private or at a church in front of a **priest**. By the mid 1100s, the Church insisted that weddings take place in front of witnesses to be sure that the couple really said "I do." Dressed in their newest, cleanest clothes, couples usually spoke their vows at the church door, the most public place in the village, town, or castle. Then, they entered the church for prayers and the priest's blessing.

▲ *Wealthy families celebrated marriages with enormous feasts and war games, called tournaments, which sometimes lasted for days.*

Widowhood

Many girls became widows at a young age because their husbands were killed in battle or tournaments, or because their husbands were much older than they were. When a woman's husband died, she received part of his property. This was called a dower. Some dowers were large enough that a woman did not have to remarry if she did not wish to, and many women remained widows. Most needed to find a new husband to support them and their children, while others entered a **convent** and dedicated their lives to God.

Housekeeping

In the late 1300s, wealthy mothers and fathers wrote books for their young daughters about how they thought a good daughter and wife should act. The instruction books also included recipes and tips on how to deal with household problems, such as getting rid of fleas. A wealthy wife probably never had to cook meals herself, but she needed to know how a dish was prepared to make sure the servants cooked it properly.

The following tips are from an instruction book written in 1392 by an elderly French merchant for his new wife, who was only fifteen years old. Her mother had died when she was very young, so no one had taught her how to run a large household.

A Good Wife ▲

A good wife is **humble** and obedient toward her husband. She is not **arrogant** and does not talk back to him in public. When her husband comes home, a good wife takes off his shoes in front of the fire, washes his feet, brings him clean shoes and socks, and serves him food and drink. She makes his bed with clean white sheets, gives him a nightcap to cover his hair, and tucks him in under warm furs. In the morning, she gives him fresh clothing.

◀ Getting Rid of Fleas

To get rid of fleas, at night spread two slices of bread with glue and **turpentine**. Place a lighted candle in the middle of each piece of bread. The fleas will come and stick there. You can also place a blanket of white wool on the bed so that you can easily see the fleas and kill them.

Recipe for Stuffed Pigling. ▶

To prepare stuffed pigling, kill the pig by cutting his throat. Plunge him in boiling water and remove his skin. Throw away the feet and **entrails** of the pig, and boil the lean meat in water.

For the stuffing, chop up the yolks of 20 hard-boiled eggs, chestnuts that have been cooked in water and peeled, some fine old cheese, and the meat of a cooked leg of pork. Cook them with plenty of **saffron** and **ginger** powder. Cut your pig open with the smallest opening you can, stuff him, sew him up with a big needle, and roast him on a **spit**.

◀ How to Behave in Public

Follow these rules for behaving in public so you do not embarrass your father or husband:

- Do not speak with anyone outside the family.
- Do not spend too much money on clothes.
- Keep your dress and shoes clean, without dirt or mud.
- Wash your face and hands and make sure they are always clean.
- Your fingernails should not be too long or full of dirt.
- Take care that drippings from your nose do not hang like icicles.
- If you have to blow your nose, use a hanky and not your fingers.
- Comb your hair and make sure that it is not full of feathers or other garbage.
- Clean your teeth and tongue.
- Do not scratch your head at the dinner table.
- Do not scratch or pick at scabs in public.
- If you must belch, do so as quietly as possible and turn your face away.

Raising a Family

Wealthy women usually had more children than poorer women because they married when they were younger, and they were healthier and less tired than peasant women who did hard labor in the fields. A wealthy woman in good health had as many as sixteen children, but most women had only two or three. Some women died from infections while giving birth because people in the Middle Ages did not know as much about germs and cleanliness as they do today.

▼ *Women had their babies at home, surrounded by their female friends and family. Men did not watch the birth or help out. A midwife, or woman whose job was to help women have babies, was sometimes present during the birth.*

Boy or Girl?

Medieval women believed there were ways of telling if a baby was going to be a boy or girl before it was born. These ways were not always accurate. They thought that if the mother walked slowly and had hollow eyes, she would have a boy. If she walked quickly and had swollen eyes, she would have a girl. They also said that if a pregnant woman was asked to choose between a lily and a rose, and she chose the lily, she would have a boy. If she chose the rose, she would have a girl.

Feeding a Baby

Peasant mothers and poorer townswomen breastfed their babies. Most wealthy mothers, especially in southern Europe, hired wet nurses instead. A wet nurse fed the lady's baby with her own milk. Medieval parents were very careful about the women they chose as a wet nurse because they believed that the wet nurse's personality could be passed to their child through the milk.

A Family's Health

Women in the Middle Ages were in charge of the health of their families and servants. They learned to heal wounds, set broken or dislocated bones, and cure diseases with medicines made from plants and herbs. Many more children died in the Middle Ages than today. As many as half died before they turned five from illnesses. Others were killed in accidents while following their parents around as they worked. In times of poor crops, many children did not get enough to eat. If girls survived until the age of twelve and boys survived until the age of fifteen, they had reached adulthood.

▲ Feeding a family was a large job for women in the Middle Ages. Women in towns shopped for food in markets and prepared meals in a fireplace. They had to carefully watch the food as it cooked to make sure it did not burn over the hot flames.

◀ Medieval mothers wrapped newborn babies tightly in strips of fabric to keep them warm. This was called swaddling. Some women believed that if they did not swaddle their babies, the babies would grow up crooked.

Women and the Church

In the Middle Ages, many girls and women dedicated their lives to the Roman Catholic Church. These women were called nuns. Nuns lived in walled communities, called convents, where they prayed, read and copied books, and sometimes taught younger girls. When entering the convent, nuns promised to obey certain rules, such as giving away all their personal belongings and having no contact with people from the outside world, unless they had permission. Most nuns were noblewomen or townswomen because only wealthier families could afford to pay for their daughters to enter the convent.

▼ *Nuns in cities dedicated their lives to healing the sick and taking care of the poor and elderly in hospitals. The smaller girls are novices who are learning how to be nuns.*

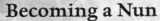

Becoming a Nun

Some women and girls became nuns because they believed strongly in their religion. Other girls became nuns to avoid marrying. Nuns were known for their great learning, so girls entered the convent to get an education. Many girls were placed in convents at a young age because their families believed it would please God, or because they could not find husbands for their daughters or afford a dowry. Widows often moved to convents after their husbands died to live quiet lives of prayer away from family duties.

▲ *Nuns prayed in the convent's church eight times a day. Nuns wore long black and white garments called habits. Wimples, which were pieces of white cloth, covered their heads and throats.*

By 1100, more and more women wished to live religious lives. There were not enough places in convents, and not all women could afford to pay to enter, so they found other ways to serve God. Women in towns and cities, called beguines, set up communities where they lived together, prayed, cared for the sick, elderly, and poor, and supported themselves by working as teachers, nurses, and clothmakers. Some wore a habit, like nuns, and others just dressed plainly.

Abbesses

The nun who ran the convent was called an abbess. Many abbesses, especially those in the early Middle Ages, became powerful, respected leaders. Not only did they supervise the nuns, but they managed the convent's land and money, which wealthy people donated.

Hildegard of Bingen (1098–1179) was a powerful, well-educated German abbess. In addition to leading her nuns, she wrote a play, a book on science and medicine, and three books that described her religious visions. These books were very influential, and popes, kings, and queens wrote to her for advice.

Educating Girls

Girls in the Middle Ages were taught by their mothers how to run a household and take care of their husband and children. At age seven, noble girls were sometimes sent to live at other noble households that were wealthier and more influential than their own. The girls became ladies-in-waiting. They served the lady of the castle and learned how to sew, embroider, sing, dance, tell stories, ride horses, and hunt.

Girls who lived in towns and cities usually learned a trade from their fathers. The poorest city girls started working for wages around the age of seven, often as servants in other families' homes. Peasant girls learned how to farm, take care of farm animals, cook, and sew by watching their mothers and older sisters.

▶ *Noble girls were taught how to read and write by their mothers. Sometimes, the castle clergyman, who was the most educated person in the household, helped teach the girls.*

Going to School

It was very difficult for a girl in the Middle Ages to get more than a basic education. Most people believed that girls did not need to be well educated, so there were few schools and women were not allowed to attend the few universities that existed. Some girls were lucky enough to have families who wanted them to get the best education possible. These families hired private tutors to teach the girls how to read and write, or they sent the girls to schools in convents. By the end of the 1300s, some girls in towns and cities who were between the ages of six and twelve attended girls' schools that were being set up and run by the Church or the city.

▼ *Girls learned skills to help them take care of a family and run a household. These girls learned to spin wool so that they could make clothing.*

Heloise

Heloise was a **scholar** born in Paris, France, who lived in the 1100s. Her uncle, who was in charge of her education after her parents died, sent her to a convent school. Then, when Heloise was seventeen, he hired Peter Abelard, one of the greatest teachers of the time, to be her private tutor. Abelard was very impressed with Heloise's intelligence, and they soon fell in love and got married.

Heloise's uncle was very angry about the marriage and hired men to beat up Abelard. Abelard placed Heloise in a convent, then made her the abbess of another convent that he founded. For the rest of her life, Heloise looked after and taught her nuns with great wisdom.

Medieval Style

In the Middle Ages, women dressed in several layers. They wore long, close-fitting underdresses, called chemises or kirtles, made of linen. On top of a chemise, they wore tunics that reached the ankle. Sometimes, a belt made from cloth or silk cord was tied around the hips. Stockings, like long socks, covered the legs from the feet to above the knees and were tied in place with laces. Shoes were made from leather.

Peasant women and some townswomen made their own clothes from cloth they wove out of coarse wool or that they bought from weavers in their village or town. The clothes of wealthy women and girls were made from fine woolen cloth woven from the softest fleece, from silk, and from other luxurious fabrics. The finest silk, called cloth of gold, had gold threads woven into it.

In the colder parts of Europe, clothes were lined with animal fur. Wealthy women wore expensive furs from animals such as Siberian squirrels and ermines, a kind of weasel. Less wealthy townswomen and peasant women lined their clothing with rabbit, cat, and badger fur, or with lambskin.

Dyeing Cloth

People in the Middle Ages colored cloth using dyes made from plants, animals, and **minerals**. Some ingredients for dyes came from far away and were very expensive. Red, yellow, blue, and brown dyes were made from plants that grew in Europe. Green, orange, and purple dyes were made by mixing these colors together.

A deeper blue was made from the indigo plant, which grew in India, and deep dark reds came from sappanwood trees in Asia. The vivid red color called crimson, worn only by nobles, was the most expensive color. It was made from a **Middle Eastern** insect called the kermes beetle that merchants brought to Europe.

Medieval Headdresses

Married women wore head coverings when they left their homes. Most women wore simple headdresses, such as a linen kerchief, which kept their hair off their face while they worked. Many noblewomen and women who lived in towns and cities covered their hair with pieces of white linen, called veils. They also wore wimples, which were pieces of fabric wrapped around the neck and pinned up under the veil so that no hair showed. This was a sign of **modesty**.

As time passed, the headdresses of wealthy women got bigger and fancier. By the 1400s, fashionable women pinned nets of silver or gold cord, called cauls or crespinettes, to each side of their head and filled them with coils of braided hair. Tall hats, called hennin, were also popular. Scarves or heavier veils often flowed from the tip of the hats as decoration.

▲ *The women in this picture are wearing different styles of hennin. Some hennin were tall and cone-shaped, while others had flat tops. The queen is wearing a fancy horn-shaped caul.*

Beauty

In the Middle Ages, fashionable women wanted to be slim with long golden hair, black eyebrows, ivory teeth, sparkling gray eyes, small lips, a long neck, and white skin.

Wealthy women made their faces pale by applying a white paint made from powder mixed with water. Unfortunately, many powders contained lead, which poisoned the women who used them. Other women had barbers, who also acted as surgeons in the Middle Ages, bleed them. The barber cut a vein in their arm and allowed enough blood to flow out that the women became pale.

▲ *Starting in the 1300s, it became fashionable to make faces look long and oval. Women plucked or shaved the hair on their foreheads to raise their hairlines. They also plucked their eyebrows into thin lines.*

Hygiene

Having a bath was a major chore in the Middle Ages because water had to be drawn from a well, heated on a fire, and then carried to the bath, which was often made from half a barrel. Most people in castles and villages had a proper bath only once in a while. In the winter, they washed themselves with a cloth dipped in a basin of water. In the summer, they bathed more regularly in lakes or streams. People in the cities bathed more often because they went to public bathhouses, where they paid a small fee to bathe.

By the 1100s, peasants and poorer city people used harsh soap made from animal fat and ashes when they washed. Wealthy people could afford gentler soap made from olive oil that came from Spain. Twigs were used to clean teeth, and people chewed on herbs, such as aniseed and mint, to freshen their breath.

Curing Skin Problems

Medieval girls and women created lotions that were supposed to make their skin look smooth. One recipe for a skin lotion said to mix asparagus roots, a wild herb called anise, and the bulbs of white lilies with the milk of donkeys and red goats. The mixture was placed in warm horse dung until it aged, then it was **filtered** through felt. Women rubbed their face with pieces of soft bread dipped in the mixture.

Beauty in Asia

Like wealthy women in western Europe, wealthy women in medieval Japan and China preferred pale skin. They painted their faces pure white, then used rouge to redden their cheeks and lips. They also shaved their eyebrows and painted on new ones. Japanese women thought the white facepaint made their teeth look yellow, so they painted their teeth black to hide them.

▶ *Japanese women styled their hair in elaborate shapes held in place by decorated sticks that looked like chopsticks.*

Footbinding

Footbinding was a Chinese custom that started in the 900s. Chinese people thought tiny feet were beautiful and showed that a girl was from a wealthy and good family. When their daughters were five or six years old, mothers bound their daughters' feet to prevent them from growing. The toes were bent underneath the feet and tied tightly in place with long, narrow cotton bandages. Over the next few years, the bandages were tightened so that eventually the girl's toes were pressed close to her heels. Some feet were only three inches long. Walking and standing was difficult and very painful.

▲ *Handmade shoes embroidered with beautiful patterns and designs were meant to show off Chinese women's tiny feet.*

Women Around the World

In the Middle Ages, life for women around the world varied depending on where they lived.

The Muslim World

In the Middle Ages, Muslims, who follow the religion of **Islam**, ruled a vast territory that included large parts of Spain, Africa, India, and most of the Middle East. The *Qur'an*, or Muslim holy book, gave Muslim women special rights. Muslim women earned money by sewing, embroidering, and weaving and dyeing silk. Women in cities bought and sold land and buildings, rented out shops to merchants, and lent money. Other women worked as midwives, bakers, singers, servants, nurses, and sellers of food, clothes, jewelry, and other small goods.

Most Muslim women married between the ages of twelve and sixteen. If they married wealthy men, their husbands sometimes had more than one wife. Muslim men were allowed to have up to four wives, as long as they treated all their wives with respect and kindness and could afford to give each of them their own house.

▲ In the mosque, which is the Muslim house of worship, women and children prayed in a separate section from men. Many Muslim women wore veils outside their homes as a sign of modesty.

Japanese Women

In Japan, daughters remained close to their parents, even after marriage. Wives of warriors known as samurai looked after their homes and raised their children, but sometimes they were also trained in the **martial arts** and helped defend their family's land in times of war. When their husbands died, noble and samurai widows were allowed to inherit their husbands' wealth and land. By the end of the Middle Ages, the role of Japanese women changed. They were expected to be silent and obey their husbands without question.

◄ *Japanese women wore beautiful, colorful silk garments called kimonos and* **geta,** *which were wooden shoes with platform soles that prevented the bottom of kimonos from getting dirty.*

Chinese Women

In medieval China, daughters were considered less important than sons. Most families thought that daughters were burdens because they needed dowries to find good husbands.

Parents arranged their daughters' marriages when their daughters were in their teens. After getting married, a girl lived with her husband's family and had very little contact with her own family. The girl's mother-in-law was in charge of the house, and the new wife was the least important member of the family. She had to obey her husband and his parents without arguing or questioning them. Many wives had to share their husbands with other wives because Chinese men were allowed to have as many wives as they could afford.

▶ *Wu Zeitan (625–705) was the only woman to ever rule China. She ruled for her husband, the emperor Kao-Tsung, when he became sick, then took over the throne from her son three years after he was named emperor.*

Famous Women

Women in the Middle Ages made important contributions to the societies in which they lived. They became writers, art collectors, doctors, healers, and warriors.

Khadija

Khadija, who lived in the late 500s and early 600s, was the wealthy widow of a merchant from the city of Mecca, in present-day Saudi Arabia. She hired Muhammad, who later became a **prophet** of Islam, to help her with her business and then married him. After Muhammad received messages from Allah, or God, telling him to teach the world about Islam, Khadija was the first person to become Muslim.

Murasaki Shikibu ▶

Murasaki Shikibu (973–1025) was a writer from a noble Japanese family. While serving as a lady-in-waiting to Empress Akiko, she wrote a popular book called *The Tale of Genji*, about an imaginary prince named Genji.

Anna Comnena

Anna Comnena (1083–1148) was the daughter of the emperor Alexius I from Constantinople, in present-day Turkey. She was the world's first known female historian. Her fifteen-book history of her family, called *Alexiad*, was full of details about daily life at court, the deeds of her family, and the **crusades**.

Eleanor of Aquitaine

Eleanor of Aquitaine (1122–1204) was one of the most powerful women of the Middle Ages. She ruled the vast region of Aquitaine, in what is now southern France, which she inherited from her father when she was only fifteen years old. She also became queen of France and then England when she married the kings of those countries. As queen, she went on a crusade and helped the king of England and two of her sons, who became kings, rule.

◀ Christine de Pizan

Christine de Pizan (1364–1430) was born in Italy, but moved to France as a child. She was the first known woman to make a living by writing books. She wrote about religion, history, and the role of women in medieval society. Her books were translated into other languages, such as English and Italian, so that people around Europe could read them.

Joan of Arc ▶

Joan of Arc (1412–1431) was a young French peasant girl who became a heroine during the Hundred Years War between France and England. When she was thirteen years old, Joan claimed to hear the voices of **saints** telling her that she would save France from the English. Dressed as a knight, she led the French army to many victories, but after a major loss, the French no longer believed that Joan could help them win the war.

When the enemy captured Joan, the French did nothing to save her. She was handed over to the Church's court of law for a trial. The court believed that she had lied about hearing the voices of saints and that she was wrong to dress like a man. In 1431, she was burned alive at the stake. In 1456, when the war was over, Joan's sentence was **annulled**, and in 1920, the Catholic Church declared Joan a saint.

Glossary

annul To make something invalid or not count

apprentice A person learning a trade by working with someone who is more experienced

arrogant Overly proud

Christianity The religion that follows the teachings of God and Jesus Christ

clergyman A religious leader

convent A walled community where people dedicated themselves to God

crusade A holy war fought by Christians against Muslims to recover the Holy Land, the area where Jesus Christ lived and died

embroider To make a design in cloth using a needle and thread

entrails The internal organs of animals or humans

filter To remove dirt or other solids from something, using a device with tiny holes that trap the solids

ginger The underground stem of a plant, used as a spice

humble Describing a person who does not act as if he or she is better than others

inherit To receive money or possessions from someone who died

Islam A religion based on the teachings of God, whom Muslims call Allah, and his prophets

manor A noble's land

martial art A sport that uses warlike techniques for self-defense and exercise

merchant A person who buys and sells goods

Middle Eastern Describing the region of southwestern Asia and northern Africa

mineral A non-living, naturally occuring substance obtained from the ground

modesty Humble or reserved in dress, behavior, and speech

plaster A mixture of lime, sand, and water used to cover ceilings and walls

priest A person who leads religious ceremonies in the Catholic Church

prophet A person who is believed to speak on behalf of God

rent Payment made by tenants to landowners for the use of land

saffron A dark yellow spice from the stamens of a flower

saint A person through whom God has performed miracles, according to the Christian Church

scholar A person who is very educated

spit A skewer or thin rod that holds meat over a fire

turpentine A strong-smelling liquid used to make paint thinner

Index

1 2 3 4 5 6 7 8 9 0   Printed in the U.S.A.   8 7 6 5 4 3